Natural Disasters Where I Live

TORNADOES

Tracy Vonder Brink

A Stingray Book

SEAHORSE PUBLISHING

Teaching Tips for Caregivers and Teachers:

This Hi-Lo book features high-interest subject matter that will appeal to all readers in intermediate and middle school grades. It may be enjoyed by students reading at or above grade level as well as by those who are looking for age-appropriate themes matched with a less challenging reading level. Hi-Lo books are ideal for ELL readers, too.

Each book appeals to a striving reader's age and maturity level. Opportunities are provided for students to read words they already know while encountering a limited number of new, high-interest vocabulary words. With these supports in place, students will read more fluently while increasing reading comprehension. Use the following suggestions to help students grow as readers.

- Encourage the student to read independently at home.
- Encourage the student to practice reading aloud.
- Encourage activities that require reading.
- Establish a regular reading time.
- Have the student write questions about what they read.

Teaching Tips for Teachers:

Before Reading

- Ask, "What do I know about this topic?"
- Ask, "What do I want to learn about this topic?"

During Reading

- Ask, "What is the author trying to teach me?"
- Ask, "How is this like something I already know?"

After Reading

- Discuss how the text features (headings, index, etc.) help with understanding the topic.
- Ask, "What interesting or fun fact did you learn?"

TABLE OF CONTENTS

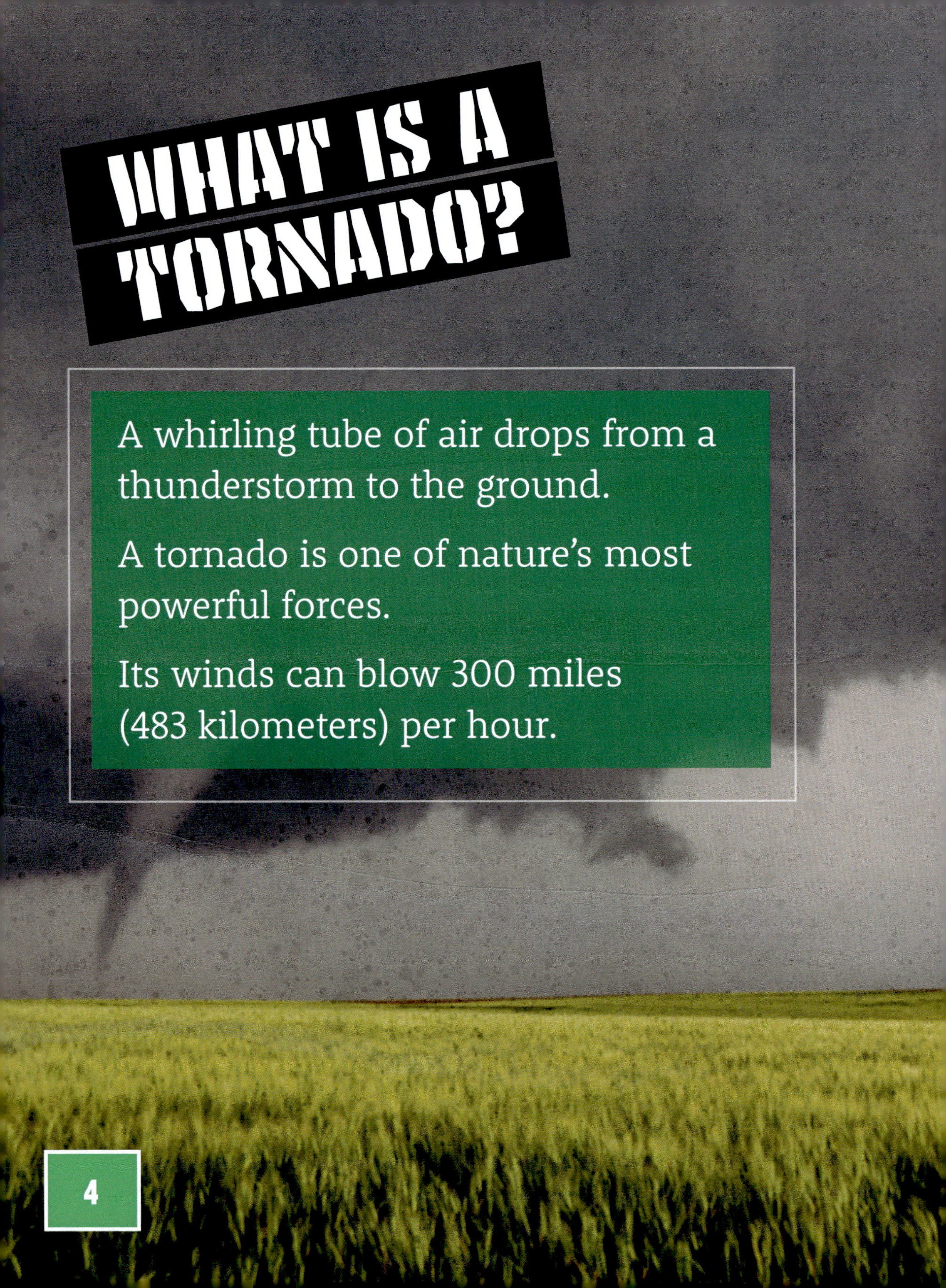

WHAT IS A TORNADO?

A whirling tube of air drops from a thunderstorm to the ground.

A tornado is one of nature's most powerful forces.

Its winds can blow 300 miles (483 kilometers) per hour.

FUNNEL FACT

Tornadoes are also called twisters, cyclones, or whirlwinds. Most last less than 10 minutes and travel only three to six miles (five to ten kilometers).

HOW DOES A TORNADO FORM?

Scientists don't completely understand how a tornado forms.

It's thought that some tornadoes begin with winds at two different heights in the air.

These winds cause air to **rotate** when they blow at different speeds.

Then, more wind blows upward. The **column** of spinning air tightens and speeds up.

Tornado Air Movement

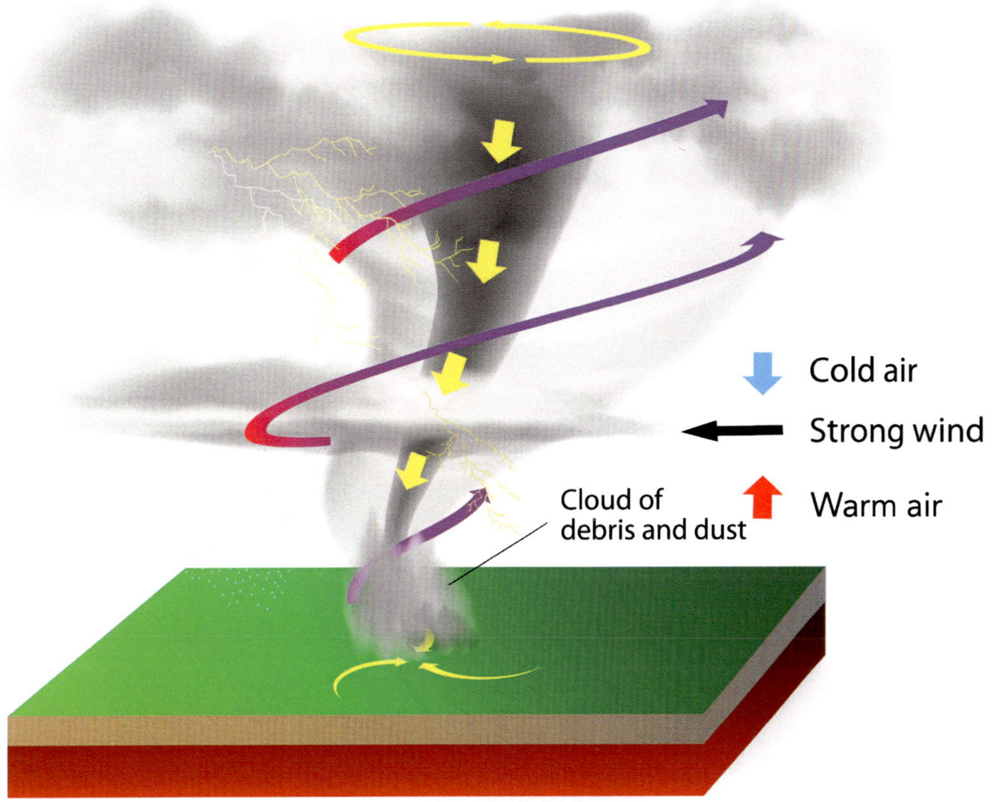

WHAT IS A FUNNEL CLOUD?

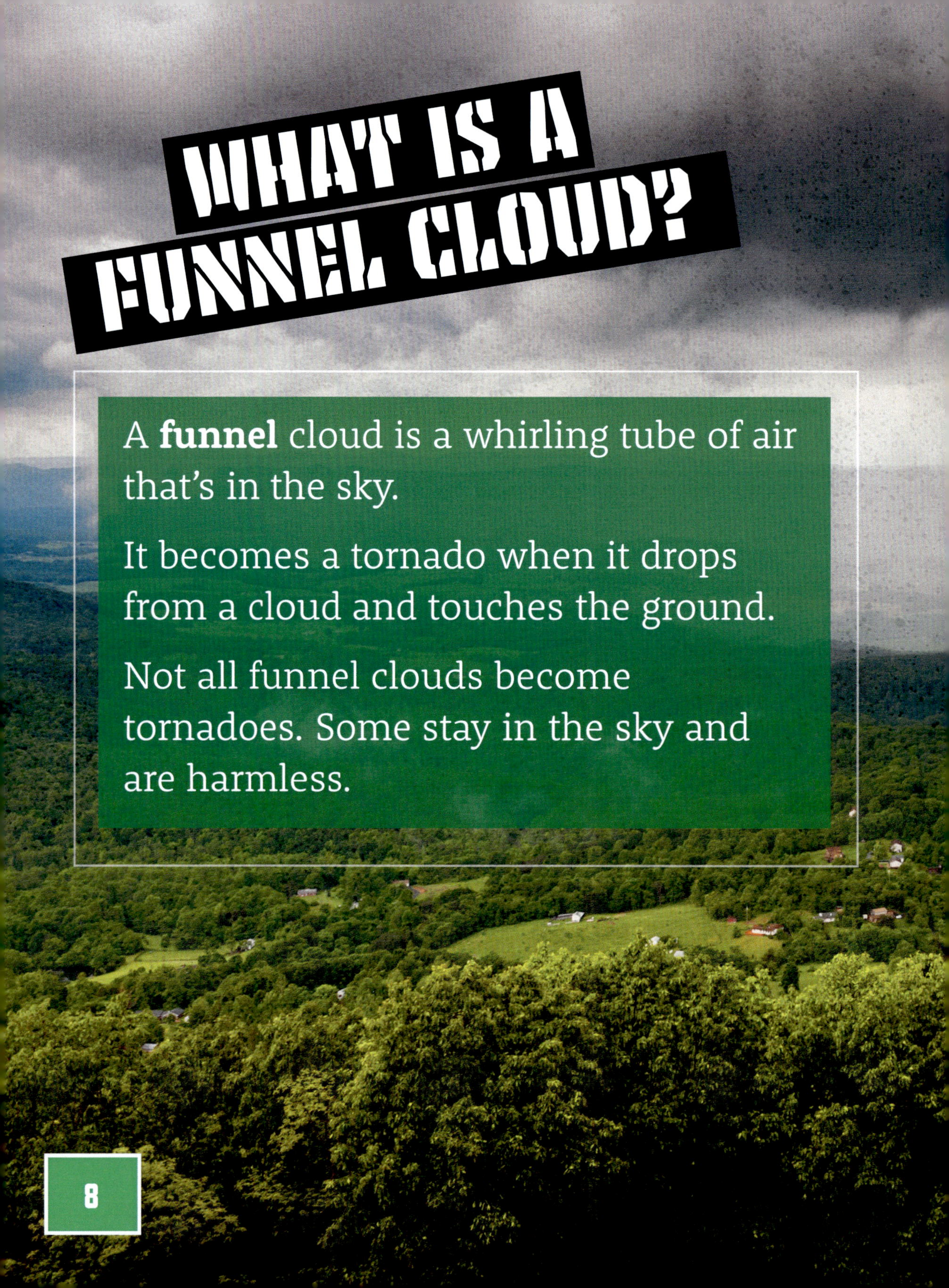

A **funnel** cloud is a whirling tube of air that's in the sky.

It becomes a tornado when it drops from a cloud and touches the ground.

Not all funnel clouds become tornadoes. Some stay in the sky and are harmless.

FUNNEL FACT

Wind is invisible, so it's hard to see a tornado until it picks up water droplets and dust.

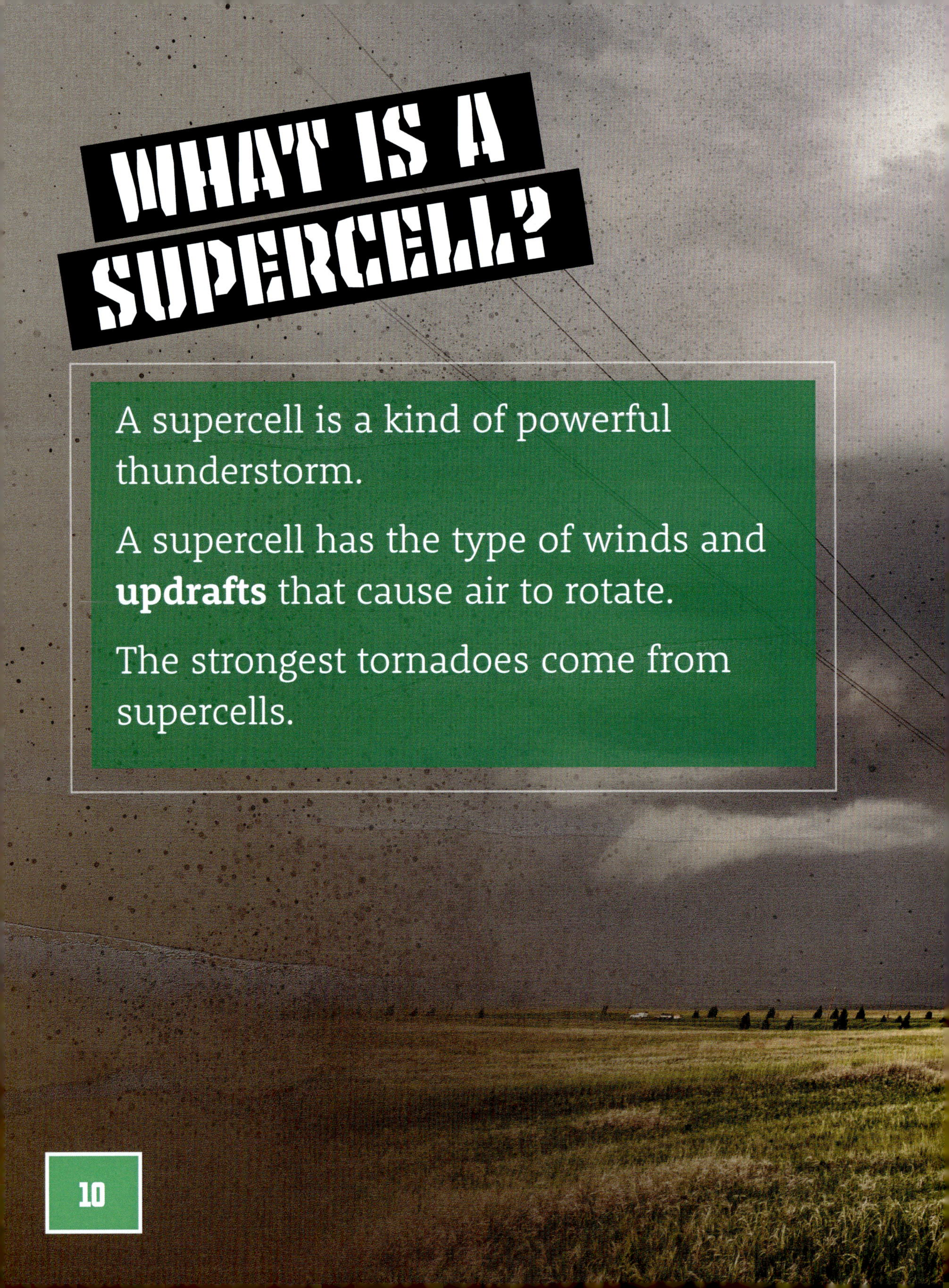

WHAT IS A SUPERCELL?

A supercell is a kind of powerful thunderstorm.

A supercell has the type of winds and **updrafts** that cause air to rotate.

The strongest tornadoes come from supercells.

FUNNEL FACT

As few as 20 percent of supercell storms produce tornadoes. Scientists don't yet understand why some do while others don't.

WHERE DO TORNADOES HAPPEN?

Tornadoes happen all over the world. They have been recorded on every continent except Antarctica.

North America has the most tornadoes.

About 1,200 tornadoes happen in the United States every year.

FUNNEL FACT

Tornadoes have been reported in all 50 states of the United States. Tornadoes can happen at any time, but most occur from 4:00 to 9:00 p.m.

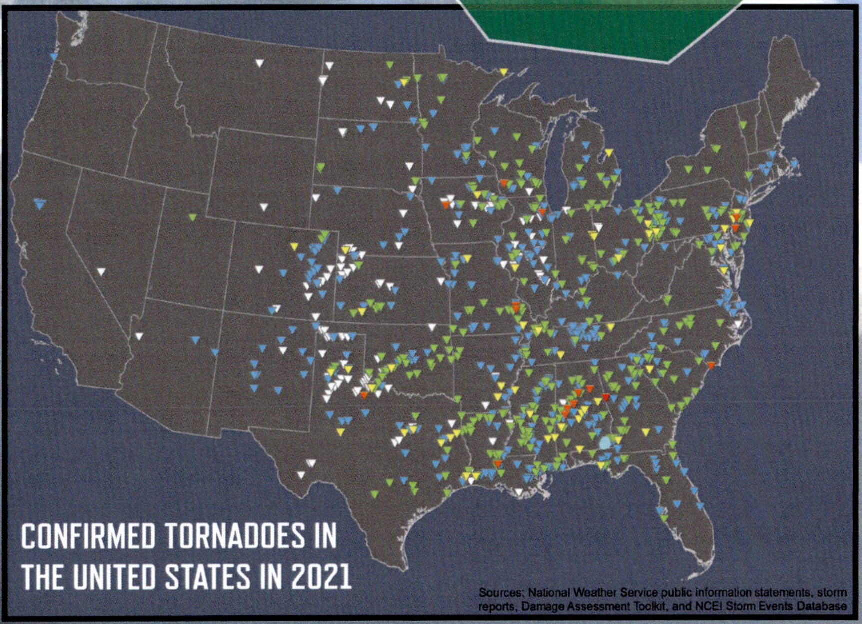

CONFIRMED TORNADOES IN THE UNITED STATES IN 2021

Sources: National Weather Service public information statements, storm reports, Damage Assessment Toolkit, and NCEI Storm Events Database

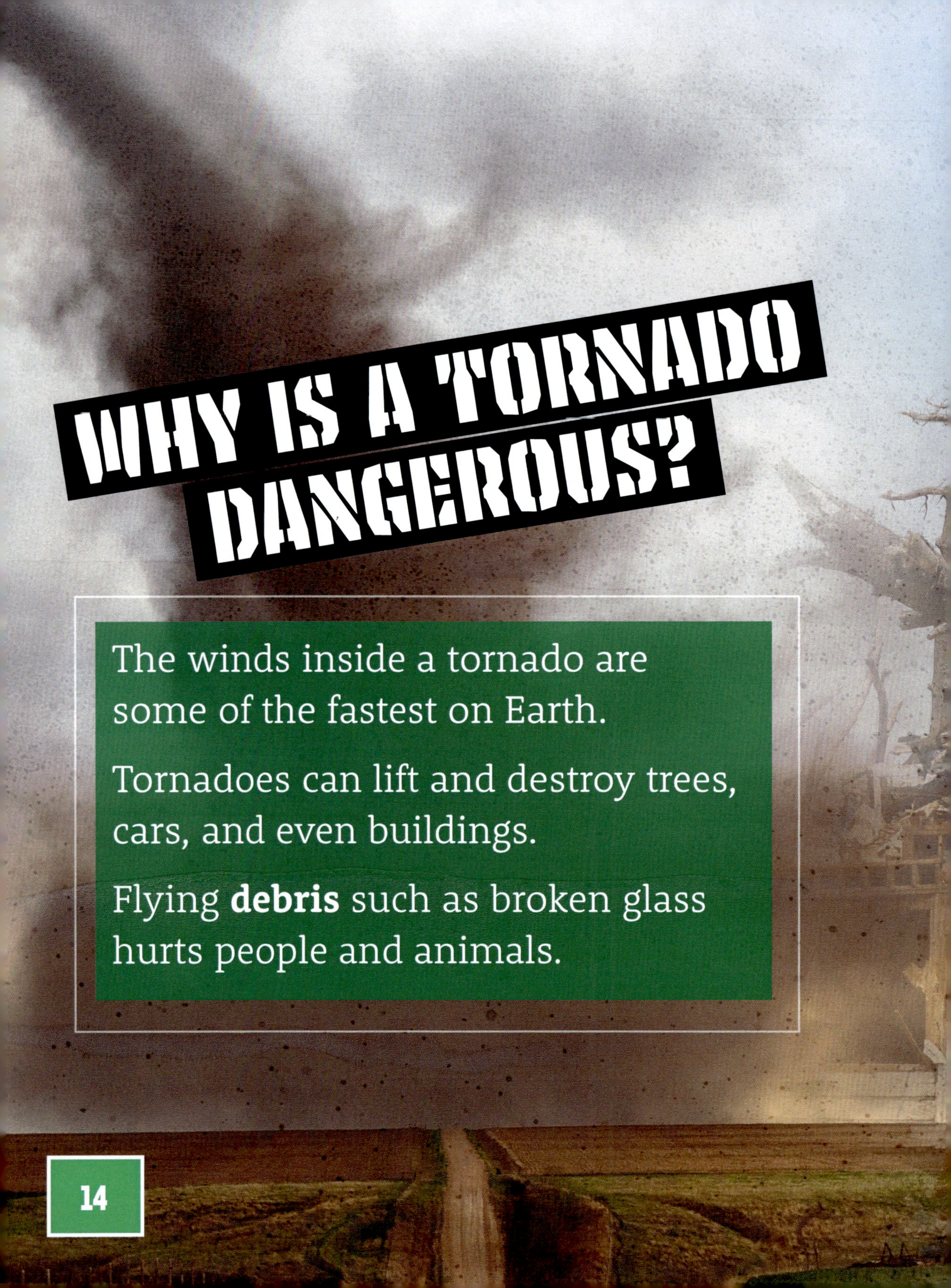

WHY IS A TORNADO DANGEROUS?

The winds inside a tornado are some of the fastest on Earth.

Tornadoes can lift and destroy trees, cars, and even buildings.

Flying **debris** such as broken glass hurts people and animals.

THE WORLD'S DEADLIEST TORNADO

A tornado struck Bangladesh in 1989.

It carved a path one mile (1.6 kilometers) wide and 10 miles (16 kilometers) long. The tornado destroyed two towns.

About 1,300 people were killed and 12,000 were injured. As many as 80,000 were left homeless after the tornado.

The Tri-State Tornado of 1925 destroyed this school in Illinois.

FUNNEL FACT

The Tri-State Tornado of 1925 was one of the deadliest in the United States. It moved through Missouri, Indiana, and Illinois, and killed 695 people.

The 1974 Super Outbreak created 148 tornadoes across 13 U.S. states.

PREDICTING A TORNADO

Doppler radar tracks thunderstorms.

Trained storm spotters on the ground report what they see.

Forecasters look at all the information and decide if a tornado is likely.

They send out a tornado watch online, on TV, and on the radio if **conditions** are right.

A tornado warning means that a tornado has touched the ground.

WEATHER
ALERT

STAYING SAFE DURING A TORNADO

Go to the basement or to an inside room without windows on the lowest floor.

Get under something sturdy. Cover your body with a blanket, sleeping bag, or mattress. Be sure to protect your head.

Find a nearby building if you are outside or in a mobile home.

If you are in a car, do not try to outrun a tornado. Leave it and find the nearest building.

Practice drills help students know what to do in case of a tornado.

GLOSSARY

column (KAH-luhm): something with a long, upright shape that is usually round

conditions (kuhn-DISH-uhnz): things that must occur before other things can occur

debris (duh-BREE): remains or pieces of something broken down or destroyed

Doppler radar (DAHP-luhr RAY-dahr): a weather tool that sends out radio waves to find out information about storms

funnel (FUHN-uhl): something shaped like a wide cone that narrows to a slender tube at the bottom

rotate (ROH-tayt): to move or turn in a circle

updrafts (UHP-drafts): upward movements of air

INDEX

AFTER READING QUESTIONS

1. When does a funnel cloud become a tornado?
2. What are supercells? How are they related to tornadoes?
3. How many tornadoes happen in the United States each year?
4. What is the difference between a tornado watch and a tornado warning?
5. What should you do if you are outside during a tornado?

About the Author

Tracy Vonder Brink loves true stories and facts. She has written more than twenty books for kids and is a contributing editor for three children's science magazines. Tracy lives in Cincinnati, Ohio, with her husband, two daughters, and two rescue dogs.

Written by: Tracy Vonder Brink
Design by: Under the Oaks Media
Editor: Kim Thompson

Photographs/Shutterstock: Minerva Studio: cover(bottom); Newtonian: cover (top); Huntstyle: p. 4-5; SingerGM: p. 6-7; NOAA: p. 6a, 16, 17; Designua: p. 7a; Jon Bilous: p. 8-9; Cammie Czuchinicki: p. 10-11; Todd Shoemake: p. 12-13; Dstie: p. 14-15; Patrick Jennings: p. 18-19; Matteo Benegiamo: p. 19; Photoguru73: p. 21

Library of Congress PCN Data
Tornadoes / Tracy Vonder Brink
Natural Disasters Where I Live
ISBN 978-1-63897-480-2(hard cover)
ISBN 978-1-63897-595-3(paperback)
ISBN 978-1-63897-710-0(EPUB)
ISBN 978-1-63897-825-1(eBook)
Library of Congress Control Number:
2021953362

Printed in Canada/092023/CPC20230911

Seahorse Publishing Company
www.seahorsepub.com

Published in the United States
Seahorse Publishing
PO Box 771325
Coral Springs, FL 33077

SEAHORSE PUBLISHING